MW01594870

In the *Fullness* of *Joy*

These things have I spoken unto you,
that my joy might remain in you,
and that your joy might be full.

John 15:11

Sherry Faircloth Skinner

Tate Publishing, LLC.

Published in the United States of America
by Tate Publishing, LLC
127 East Trade Center Terrace
Mustang, OK 73064
(888) 361–9473

Scripture quotations marked "KJV" are taken from the
Holy Bible, King James Version, Cambridge, 1769.

ISBN: 1-5988630-9-6

For our precious Lord Jesus,

"The joy of my life."

Acknowledgments

I am grateful for the love and support of my family, Marvin Skinner, David Skinner, Daniel and Lisa Skinner, and Wade and Elizabeth Grimm. May God richly bless you for your willing assistance in bringing this book to completion.

A special "thank you" to Tate Publishing for a warm response to my work, and for their expertise in the world of publishing. I knew my search for a publisher was over when I read their established Word from the scriptures, *"The Lord gave some a Word; great was the company of those that published it."* (Psalm 68:11)

Table of Contents

Foreword

Poetry. A language, I believe, that only a few of us can truly grasp, comprehend, and appreciate. Oh sure, many enjoy reading poetry, but I am talking about those blessed and gifted persons that God has truly adorned with the gift of writing poetry. My mother is one of those persons. She gives us a taste of this blessing bestowed upon her from God with *In the Fullness of Joy.* For the reader, the words on these pages are simply a gift from God. And, my mother will fully attest that her writings are awe-inspired words from our Heavenly Father. Yes, she wrote them, but, if asked, she would immediately reply that these words are inspirations from God. Couple her humility with her desire to introduce the lost, troubled, and despondent to our Lord and Savior Jesus Christ and you come up with the poems reflected on these pages. In her own words in introducing this book, she pleads that these writings will lead others to join together their lighted candles so as to "brighten a dark world." Well, this book is a sweet-smelling burning candle!

Dan Skinner

Introduction

I am so thankful to live in America. The most important thing to know about America is that it is about ordinary people, living ordinary lives, doing extraordinary things, praying simple prayers. This is what has made our country great.

You may be surprised to learn that people are not only praying in churches, but in our schools and colleges, offices and plants, our sports arenas, our military, our hospitals, in our judicial system and the media. People are making a difference with prayer, helping to keep our nation strong as we journey on toward home, leaving behind a godly legacy for future generations.

Do we still have a good and a great nation? As sure and true as our Father in heaven, the source of what is good and great. We have a promise from God that if He begins a good work in us, He will not complete it until the day of the Lord. (Philippians 1:6) God began a good work in the early praying Americans who bravely settled in this land. This is God's country and God will prevail!

I am an ordinary person, living an ordinary life who prayed a simple prayer. I asked God to allow me to light a candle and shine His light for ones who have not come to know Him; living sad, lonely, and confused lives. My prayer is to join the lighted candles shining every where, and for others to come and light a candle so that together our lights will shine forth to brighten a dark world.

Let us be children of the light, for Christ said, Ye are the light of the world. A city that is set on an hill cannot be hid. Neither do men light a candle, and put it under a bushel, but on a candlestick; and it giveth light unto all that are in the house. Let your light so shine before men, that they may see your good works, and glorify your Father which is in heaven.

(Matthew 5:14–16)

Sherry Faircloth Skinner

Psalm 16

Preserve me, O God:
for in thee do I put my trust.
O my soul, thou hast said unto the
LORD, Thou art my LORD: my
goodness extendeth not to thee; But to
the saints that are in the earth,
and to the excellent,
in whom is all my delight.
Their sorrows shall be multiplied that
hasten after another god:
their drink offerings of blood
will I not offer,
nor take up their names into my lips.
The LORD is the portion of mine
inheritance and of my cup: thou
maintainest my lot.
The lines are fallen unto me in pleasant
places; yea, I have a goodly heritage.
I will bless the LORD, who hath given
me counsel: my reins also
instruct me in the night seasons.
I have set the LORD always before me:
because he is at my right hand,
I shall not be moved.
Therefore my heart is glad, and my glory

rejoiceth: my flesh also shall rest in hope.
For thou wilt not leave my soul in hell;
neither wilt thou
suffer thine Holy One to see corruption.

Thou wilt shew me the path of life:
in thy presence is fullness of joy;
at thy right hand there are
pleasures for evermore.

God's Hand is in Everything

God's hand is in everything
Let Him paint the story,
He does it so well
With grandeur and glory.
Blending in rainbows, sunrises, sunsets,
HE CAN
With the merest touch of His hand
Color our mornings, our evenings,
our nights,
Dazzle in color our dreams of His light.
Lighting shadows of darkness
Heightening form to our trees
Mingles blues to the oceans
Greens to the seas.
He changes our seasons with a touch of
His hand
He selects the color as no human can
White to the snowflakes
Glisten to the rain
Gold to the deserts
Tan to the plains.
Dripping shades of dewdrops
Splashing boldly to flowers

Delighting our eyes
How He fills the hours.
Oh, the joy He sends us
As we know of His hand
As He spectacularly brushes the land,
IT IS
An honor to place
My hand
IN HIS.

"Blessed be the LORD,
who daily loadeth us with benefits,
even the God of our salvation."

Psalm 68:19

First Light

In the night of a storm
In the throes of despair,
We whisper, God listens
He touches with care.
For there is no darkness
God's love won't penetrate,
No fear too strong
His hand will not break.
He's walking toward us
Has seen all before,
Watch through the darkness
For His searchlight of joy.
For God moves in small ways
And bigger ways, too
And when we're most helpless
His light will break through.
So let us never
Bow to the storm
It was out of the darkness
God's light first was born.

" . . . Awake thou that sleepest,
and arise from the dead,
and Christ shall give thee light."

Ephesians 5:14

Psalm 24

The earth is the LORD'S,
and the fullness thereof;
the world, and they that dwell therein.
For he hath founded it upon the seas,
and established it upon the floods.
Who shall ascend into
the hill of the LORD?
Or who shall stand in his holy place?
He that hath clean hands,
and a pure heart;
who hath not lifted up
his soul unto vanity,
nor sworn deceitfully.
He shall receive the
blessing from the LORD,
and righteousness from
the God of his salvation.
This is the generation of them
that seek him,
that seek thy face, O Jacob.
Lift up your heads, O ye gates; and be ye
lift up, ye everlasting doors;
and the King of glory shall come in.
Who is the King of glory?
The LORD strong and mighty,

the LORD mighty in battle.
Lift up your heads, O ye gates;
even lift them up,
ye everlasting doors;
and the King of glory shall come in.
Who is this King of glory?
The LORD of hosts,
he is the King of glory.

A True Connection

The world cannot assure me
My God is real,
It is here in my heart
That I know how I feel.
I need not listen
To a worldly view,
For my God's love
Reveals He is true.
It is here in my heart
A richness is growing,
This world cannot offer
A love that's all-knowing.
Of a true connection
To one greater than man,
How great is the wondrous
True touch of His hand.
I've seen in my vision
The stars and the trees,
And I've heard the sound
From the rolling seas.
I've touched the flowers
Drawn from deepest dark sod,
But it is here in my heart
That I truly know God.

*"Keep thy heart with all diligence;
for out of it are the issues of life."*

Proverbs 4:23

Joyful Sprinkles

The little flower stood alone
As sad as it could be,
For all around was nothingness
As far as it could see.
Then from the sky a little bee
Came buzzing 'round its head,
Touched the loneliness with nectar
A lovely floral bloom was fed.
And the loneliness was banished
With a gentle blowing breeze,
Which brought along a visit
From the golden falling leaves.
And the glowing of the sunshine
Stopped by awhile to see,
And the coolness of a shower
Made it bow its head with glee.
Amid the joyful sprinkles
The little flower came to see,
It was not alone at all
Only thought the way things be.

*"I will not leave you comfortless;
I will come to you."*

John 14:18

In All Thy Ways

Needful of the ways of You
Lord, move in closer, still
I long so for a mountain view
While I linger on a hill.
More of You I aim to see
As I know You more and more,
And I yearn to be like You
As I never have before.
I want your stillness in my anger
Your compassion in my tears,
Your love to grant forgiveness
Calm in the heart of fear.
I want to know Your patience
When evil darts are flying free,
My prayer to You this day, O Lord
Let me be more like Thee.

*"In all thy ways acknowledge him,
and he shall direct thy paths."*

Proverbs 3:6

Greater Is He

In pursuit of perfection
As God's goodness comes through,
Let us bow to His glory
In all that we do.
Rise unto His greatness
He lets us be bold,
And we're never too young
Too small or too old.
Be strong and have courage
And take a right stand,
And let us forget not
The strength of His hand.
He will help us to remember
As we daily grow,
The truth of His presence
We've come to know.
Our hearts will sing praises
To His glory on view,
As God lets us know
His greatness is true.

*"And he arose, and rebuked the wind,
and said unto the sea, Peace, be still.
And the wind ceased,
and there was a great calm."*

Mark 4:39

Forever Joy

Lord, keep me from tomorrow's troubles
Let me trust in You today,
Let me stand upon Your promises
Keep You in my heart to stay.
You are here in every happening
In the life You've granted me,
With a reason and a purpose
In all I do and all I see.
Let me know good changes come
From all the sorrows that I see,
When I come to realize
Change within the heart of me.
Your love is freely given
And with opened eyes I'll see,
Your joy will last forever
And for all eternity.

"Sorrow is better than laughter:
for by the sadness of the countenance
the heart is made better."

Ecclesiastes 7:3

Psalm 98

O SING unto the LORD a new song;
for he hath done marvelous things:
his right hand, and his holy arm,
hath gotten him the victory.
The LORD hath made
known his salvation:
his righteousness hath he openly shewed
in the sight of the heathen.
He hath remembered his mercy and his
truth toward the house of Israel: all the
ends of the earth have seen
the salvation of our God.
Make a joyful noise unto the LORD,
all the earth: make a loud noise,
and rejoice, and sing praise.
Sing unto the LORD with the harp;
with the harp, and the voice of a psalm.
With trumpets and sound of cornet make
a joyful noise before the LORD,
the King.
Let the sea roar, and the fullness thereof;
the world, and they that dwell therein.
Let the floods clap their hands:
let the hills be joyful together
Before the LORD;

for he cometh to judge the earth:
with righteousness shall he
judge the world,
and the people with equity.

A Maze of Color

I faced a maze of color
When I was a four-year-old,
There's red and yellow, black and white
A kindly teacher told.
She told God loves us everyone
We are precious in His sight,
God loves all children 'round the world
No matter dark or light.
I gazed at the pretty colors
Tucked in a box so bright,
To see ones in these colors
Will that give me a fright?
I touched the pretty colors
One-by-one I tested me,
Not a single color in the box
Could match the skin of me.
In perplexity I fretted
In puzzlement I frowned,
Lord, did you forget me
I'm not red or white or brown?
Mom and Dad were at a loss
To know what bothered me,
For the little load I carried
Was far too big to see.
A kind and loving Granddad

Tried to see what he could see,
He took the time for a saddened child
And placed me on his knee.
He told the colors of the crayons
Are made by the hand of man,
And the colors of the human race
Are made by our God's hand.
Don't place your eyes on crayons
Place on our Father, high
A quieting heart responded
With deepest, calming sigh.
With gentleness and kindness
He tucked me into bed,
I'm reminded of a saying
A wisely noble said.
Don't let yourself be fretful
For when all is said and done,
"God loves each one of us as
if we are only one."

*"But Jesus said, Suffer little children,
and forbid them not, to come unto me:
for of such is the kingdom of heaven."*

Matthew 19:14

A Place for Me

Lord, You placed the sun high in the sky
The moon is where You need it be,
You fill the streams and rivers
You control the mighty sea.
The little birds are singing
From high aloft the trees,
The desert finds its reason
The wild are roaming free.
My soul waits thou upon Thee
My expectations come from You,
I adore all You have shown me
Thy great hand is in my view.
The mountains stand majestically
And the stars I nightly see,
I know that in Your grand design
There is a place for me.

"The steps of a good man are ordered
by the LORD:
and he delighteth in his way."

Psalm 37:23

Our Thankful Hearts

Lord, let us meet with gladness
Each day that You bring,
With joy in our hearts
And praises to sing.
Bring forth Your blessings
All our hearts can hold,
To share with others
In a world that's grown cold.
Let us be strong with great courage
Keep us unafraid,
As we let others know
The CHOICE that we made,
Fills hearts that are lonely
Soothes souls found in pain,
Brings an uplifting spirit
To walk tall again.
For we knew the world
Yet, our hearts sought You,
Let our thankful hearts
Greet a day made brand new.

*"Now unto him that is able to
keep you from falling,
and to present you faultless before the presence
of his glory with exceeding joy,"*

Jude 1:24

Psalm 1

Blessed is the man that walketh not in the
counsel of the ungodly, nor standeth in the
way of sinners, nor sitteth in the
seat of the scornful.
But his delight is in the law of the LORD;
and in his law doth he
meditate day and night.
And he shall be like a tree planted by the
rivers of water, that bringeth forth
his fruit in his season;
his leaf also shall not wither; and
whatsoever he doeth shall prosper. The
ungodly are not so: but are like the chaff
which the wind driveth away.
Therefore the ungodly shall not stand
in the judgment, nor sinners in the
congregation of the righteous. For the
LORD knoweth the way of the righteous:
but the way of the ungodly shall perish.

Lamplighter

Lord, count me worthy of Your calling
Keep me gentle, good and kind,
Grant Your rest unto my spirit
And Your peace unto my mind.
Grant inner newness to my heart
Keep me humble as I go,
Let me glorify Your holy name
As more of You I come to know.
Cast Your might upon my pathway
From Your ever burning light,
Far brighter than the morning
Shining forth both day and night.
Grant unto me sure knowledge
Of Your love, Your will, Your way,
Let me share Your flame with others
As You shine Your light each day.
Make me Your lamplighter
Ever faithful, ever true,
Grant unto me Your wisdom
Let me grow to be like You.

"And he said unto them,
Go ye into all the world,
and preach the gospel to every creature."

Mark 16:15

On My Mind

On my mind are thoughts of Jesus
His heart beats in my soul,
My Friend and my Redeemer
Here to cherish and to hold.
Treasured thoughts of His love
From His heart into mine,
Alive with grace and mercy
Brightly does His love light shine.
He took an empty heart of mine
And filled it to the brim,
He walked me from the shadows
Gave me loving thoughts of Him.
His love has brought His Word to me
In my heart He lets me feel,
The comfort He has promised all
Is clear, is true, is real.
He let my thoughts become aware
He was with me from the start,
He is alive in truth within me
And in my heart to never part.

" . . . If ye continue in my word,
then are ye my disciples indeed;
And ye shall know the truth
and the truth shall make you free."

John 8:31–32

47

Bless the Little Children

Bless the little children with
Your hand to hold
As the horrors of reality around
them unfold,
The confusion, the chaos,
mistrust everywhere
Bless the little children, Lord,
as You hear our prayer.
Bless them as no answers are
there in the home
Where guidance and leadership
must be shown,
Give them direction, show them You care
Bless the little children, Lord,
as You hear our prayer.
Bless them as You open so wide Your arms
As each of them show us
such special charms,
We must let them hear
and make them aware
Bless the little children, Lord,
as You hear our prayer.
Bless them as we hear so
many of them shout
Someone please tell me what

this world's about,
Show them Your kindness,
show them Your way
Bless the little children,
Lord, hear us today.

"And it shall come to pass,
that before they call,
I will answer;
and while they are yet speaking,
I will hear."

Isaiah 65:24

God's Will I Pray

A little prayer to heaven
Lets me know I'm not alone,
And it only takes a moment
To fill my soul with song.
When I feel a prayer's unanswered
I think I prayed all wrong,
And feel I sought a selfish need
I find it isn't long,
Till I begin to understand
God looked into my heart,
He understood before I prayed
And listened from the start.
He just knew His way was better
Than the way I asked in prayer,
He kept me still to listen
And I did not pray in err.
When I see His answers
As I come to know His way,
It is then I understand
It is best God's will I pray.

*"Commit thy way unto the LORD;
trust also in him;
and he shall bring it to pass."*

Psalm 37:5

What a Beautiful Jesus

What a beautiful Jesus
I have met along the way,
What a glorious spirit
Who hears me when I pray.
What a wondrous dawning
When I begin my day,
What a beautiful Jesus
Here in my heart to stay.
I have heard all about
The Cross He bore for me,
I have come to know how
He died to make me free.
I have heard the good news
Of His kind and gentle ways,
And I welcome His closeness
His warmth to my days.
I will always love Jesus
For I know that He loves me,
I know He forgives all
The wrongs in me I see.
I know of His guidance
As He rights and cleanses me,
He teaches me daily
How to walk in His victory.
How grand He will help me

Do all things that I must do,
So I may please Him
Each day that I walk through.
What a beautiful Jesus
Who has made a place for me
To dwell in His presence
For all eternity.

*"I will give thee thanks in the great
congregation: I will praise thee
among much people."*

Psalm 35:18

Psalm 67

God be merciful unto us, and bless us;
and cause his face to shine upon us;
That thy way may be known upon earth,
thy saving health among all nations.
Let the people praise thee, O God;
let all the people praise thee.
O let the nations be glad and sing for joy:
for thou shalt judge the people
righteously, and govern the
nations upon earth.
Let the people praise thee, O God;
let all the people praise thee.
Then shall the earth yield
her increase; and God,
even our own God, shall bless us.
God shall bless us;
and all the ends of the earth
shall fear him.

A Day's Springtime

In the newness of morning
In the soft early light
A day's fresh beginning
Awakes from the night.
Unleashed to the glory
Of all God will bring
On the dawn of the morning
The day's season of spring.
For each day has its seasons
Like man's inner soul
To blend with mankind
Communion to hold.
And all God's creation
Has reason to be
A meaningful purpose
That our God can see.
God abides in day's springtime
Day's evening, day's night
To awaken all souls
To His glory of light.
There was a first day
All creation began
There is a midday, an ending
All there in God's hand.

" . . . I am Alpha and Omega,
the beginning and the end.

I will give unto him that is athirst of
the fountain of the water of life freely."

Revelation 21:6

Psalm 30

I will extol thee, O LORD;
for thou hast lifted me up,
and hast not made my foes to
rejoice over me.
O LORD my God, I cried unto thee,
and thou hast healed me.
O LORD, thou hast brought up my soul
from the grave: thou hast kept me alive,
that I should not go down to the pit.
Sing unto the LORD, O ye saints of his,
and give thanks at the remembrance
of his holiness.
For his anger endureth but a moment;
in his favour is life:
weeping may endure for a night,
but joy cometh in the morning.
And in my prosperity I said,
I shall never be moved.
LORD, by thy favour thou hast made my
mountain to stand strong:
thou didst hide thy face,
and I was troubled.
I cried to thee, O LORD,
and unto the LORD I made supplication.
What profit is there in my blood,
when I go down to the pit?
Shall the dust praise thee?
Shall it declare thy truth?
Hear, O LORD, and have mercy upon
me: LORD,

be thou my helper.
Thou hast turned for me my mourning
into dancing: thou hast put
off my sackcloth,
and girded me with gladness;
To the end that my glory may
sing praise to thee,
and not be silent.
O LORD my God,
I will give thanks unto thee for ever.

Let Me Walk God's Way

Let me walk a little slower
With my Lord,
Let me have my heart and soul
In one accord.
Let me savor His sweet presence
Know His kind and soft, still voice,
Feel His awesome hand of power
As my heart and soul rejoice.
Yes, let me walk a little slower
With my Lord,
Keep my eyes upon the joy
Of His reward.
Let His gentleness surround me
As I rise to greet His day,
To bring meaning to each moment
Let me walk God's Holy Way.

"O love the LORD, all ye his saints;
for the LORD preserveth the faithful,
and plentifully rewardeth the proud doer.
Be of good courage, and he shall strengthen
your heart, all ye that hope in the LORD."

Psalm 31:23–24

My Garden

Lord, I planted my garden
With love and care,
I wanted to find not
A weed anywhere.
My, do they spring up
Naught what I do,
I have my gloves on
But I'll need help from You.
It seems when I pull one
I see then, two more,
And many times asked
What is all the work for,
Then I see rosebuds
Flowers full bloom,
The tiniest of sprouts
And others to prune.
And I know little seeds
Are there 'neath the ground,
Awaiting arrival
A delight to be found.
So, Lord, I'll keep pulling
Because I know
Your beauty awaits
When You help me hoe!

"Then shall the earth yield her increase;
and God, even our own God, shall bless us."

Psalm 67:6

A Divine Connection

Lord, help me always to remember
You're forever by my side,
That I cannot wander from Your presence
When in my heart Your love abides.
Help me to ignore all my tomorrows
For a walk with You this day,
And to know that You and I together
Walk through all that comes my way.
To know life is divinely given
A most precious gift from You,
That my life and love and being
Began the day I chose to do,
All that You have taught me
From Your wisdom wide and deep,
And to live all of Your commandments
With help from promises You keep.
Grant me a divine connection
So my eyes this day will see,
And my ears will ever hear
The greatness of YOUR MAJESTY!

"Thine, O LORD, is the greatness,
and the power, and the glory, and the victory,
and the majesty: for all that is in the heaven

and in the earth is thine; thine is the kingdom,
O LORD,
and thou art exalted as head above all."

1 Chronicles 29:11

Light Upon the Day

God's voice is in the thunder
His way is in the sea,
His mercy reigns upon the earth
Poured out to you and me.
When it is troublesome to understand
What we daily hear and see,
We know His might is working
And His control will ever be.
He gives warning in His Holy Word
When it is evil we embrace,
If we refuse to listen
And ignore His amazing grace.
We lean not unto our understanding
For God is able in His way,
To bring about the nighttime
Cast light upon the day.
He is alive there in the wilderness
He is known upon a hill,
Each steppingstone is carefully laid
With love He guides His will.
Commit thy way unto His path
And delight in our Lord's way,
Acknowledge Him in all thy ways
See His love shine through each day.

*"And the work of righteousness shall be peace;
and the effect of righteousness quietness
and assurance for ever."*

Isaiah 32:17

God Holds the Cloud

You hold the silver lining
How often it is said,
You hold the dream, a soft pillow
To lay down our head.
You let us see You
As You reign there so high,
As we lift our eyes
And see rain from the sky.
You hold for the earth
In the gray pail of Yours,
Moisture so needed
As we close our doors.
You water the grasses
Give drink to the flowers,
You pour out to mountains
Filling streams for hours.
You cleanse the trees
Clear dust from the air,
You don't forget the gardens
Left in Your care.
We're told You will soften
Our tresses we style,
Splash away our tears
Leave our faces with smile.
As a dark cloud threatens

We frown with such scorn,
When You're simply warning
Of an oncoming storm.
And suddenly it's over
The good deeds are done,
You've stowed away the cloud
Made room for the sun.
As you freshen the earth
We must say it out loud,
We can rely on God's work
God holds the cloud.

*"The LORD by wisdom hath
founded the earth;
by understanding hath he
established the heavens.
By his knowledge the depths are broken up,
and the clouds drop down the dew."*

Proverbs 3:19–20

A Will to Do

When it is God you want to please
Yet, you do not think you can,
You feel you are forgotten
Feel not the movement of His hand.
When you aim and feel you failed
In everything you do,
You seek His will and purpose
His light to come shining through.
Come and know He's ever near
And you come to understand,
The desire you have to please Him
Comes forth divinely from His hand.

*"For it is God which worketh in
you both to will
and to do of his good pleasure."*

Philippians 2:13

I Remember

Our Father in heaven
Today hear my prayer,
Come take my worries
And place in Your care.
I know You can hear me
I know You can see,
And I know You care
What is happening to me.
I know You are real
I know Your Word is true,
I remember You've heard me
And I've heard from You.

"O continue thy lovingkindness unto
them that know thee;
and thy righteousness to the upright in heart."

Psalm 36:10

Psalm 103

Bless the LORD, O my soul:
and all that is within me,
bless his holy name.
Bless the LORD, O my soul,
and forget not all his benefits:
Who forgiveth all thine iniquities;
who healeth all thy diseases;
Who redeemeth thy life from destruction;
who crowneth thee with loving kindness
and tender mercies;
Who satisfieth thy mouth
with good things;
so that thy youth is renewed
like the eagle's.
The LORD executeth righteousness
and judgment for all that are oppressed.
He made known his ways unto Moses,
his acts unto the children of Israel.
The LORD is merciful and gracious,
slow to anger, and plenteous in mercy.
He will not always chide:
neither will he keep his anger for ever.
He hath not dealt with us after our sins;
nor rewarded us according
to our iniquities.

For as the heaven is high above the earth,
so great is his mercy toward
them that fear him.
As far as the east is from the west,
so far hath he removed our
transgressions from us.
Like as a father pitieth his children,
so the LORD pitieth them that fear him.
For he knoweth our frame;
he remembereth that we are dust.
As for man, his days are as grass:
as a flower of the field, so he flourisheth.
For the wind passeth over it,
and it is gone;
and the place thereof shall know
it no more.
But the mercy of the LORD is from
everlasting to everlasting upon
them that fear him,
and his righteousness unto
children's children;
To such as keep his covenant,
and to those that remember his
commandments to do them.
The LORD hath prepared his
throne in the heavens;
and his kingdom ruleth over all.
Bless the LORD, ye his angels,

that excel in strength,
that do his commandments,
hearkening unto the voice of his word.
Bless ye the LORD, all ye his hosts;
ye ministers of his, that do his pleasure.
Bless the LORD,
all his works in all places of his dominion:
bless the LORD, O my soul.

Triumph O'er Defeat

Sorrow came into my life
Assuming full control,
Weeping eyes that could not see
Relinquished heart and soul.
From a lack of understanding
I let the sorrow be,
My thoughts not focused on my Lord
For where on earth was He-
He was standing there beside me
Waiting patiently,
To let my thoughts remember
He has not forsaken me.
He gave me time to quietly listen
And to slowly dry my tears,
To remind me that He understood
And He would calm my fears.
Yes, again, He let me see
His promises are true,
And just as He did yesterday
He will forever do.
Again, I held onto His hand
To rise upon my feet,
With focused eyes upon His light
To triumph o'er defeat.
Once again He let me know

I could not make it on my own
Again, He let me feel
The greatest love that's ever known.
Again, I understood the words
From Jesus Christ the Son,
Follow me and trust me
And let my will be done.

"Rejoice not against me, O mine enemy:
when I fall,
I shall arise; when I sit in darkness,
the LORD shall be a light unto me."

Micah 7:8

Attitude

When God controls our attitude
There's naught we cannot do,
Though man can make a stab at things
It is God to see us through.
He knows the doors to open
And He knows the doors to close,
And those of us who pause and knock
It is our God who knows.
He takes the time to listen
When our spirit needs His healing,
He knows the help to offer
When it is pain our soul is feeling.
It is God who makes a perfect way
And reaches forth to hold our hand,
He teaches nothing is impossible
And lets us simply say we can.
It is God who makes each special
It is God who makes us wise,
When in need to change an attitude
It is to God we raise our eyes.

*"Wait on the LORD: be of good courage,
and he shall strengthen thine heart: wait,
I say, on the LORD."*

Psalm 27:14

Share the Light

Let us shine our light in the darkness
A beacon to all who are lost,
Many are tired on the voyage of life
Windswept, battered and tossed.
Lost in a storm of confusion
Wondering which way to turn,
For there ahead is no anchor
To grasp and to hold ever firm.
In need of a clear, strong foundation
Footsteps made steady and sure,
A need to hear the way of the truth
In need of a love right and pure.
A light that's ever brighter
Warmer and richer each day,
Fueled by the love of Our Savior
To guide in Truth on the way.
Let us share the light of the Savior
Bring a cloak of warmth to the cold,
For Christ is Truth everlasting
A light to forever hold.

"For God has not given us a spirit of fear;
but of power, and of love, and of a sound mind."

II Timothy 1:7

Fragrant Flowers

Little children everywhere
God sees on earth below,
And He loves them everyone
And each heart does know.
They are His fragrant little flowers
He placed down here to grow,
To bloom in earthly splendor
And to let His love light show.
Some grow in gardens well tended
Nurtured with care ever slow,
While others on hillsides and byways
Like wildflowers free dancing below.
His eye is ever upon them
As each learn in a different way,
Each offering their own touch of beauty
To bring us life's richest bouquet.

*"Flowers may beckon toward us,
but speak toward Heaven and God."*

Henry Ward Beecher

A Joyful Union

(In memory of Reverend E.T. Corbin)

A song needs words and music
A piano, two hands as one,
It is then the joy of a melody
Begins though the song is not sung.
With practice the song comes together
And soon the melody is done,
A harmony blending together
A joyful union begun.
Others soon hear the melody
The notes shared day by day,
We hear the beautiful music
And thank God for sending our way.
We hear God's tune in harmony
Sung through the years of time,
Through all the highs and all the lows
His presence, His love divine.
With freedom to walk,
to care and to share
Through the laughter and the tears,
Freedom to know His hand is true
As He guides us through the years.
Freedom to know the music God sends
Lets us live and love and grow,

And to learn that the greatest of blessings
Is our God we've come to know.

*"When we remove our eyes from God's great
concert of life, we hit a sour note."*

Sherry Faircloth Skinner

The Shepherd of the Hills

Take your burdens to the Lord
And leave them there,
Take your heart and place it
Safely in His care,
He is mighty, He is great
Let His Word come penetrate,
It is then your burdens
He will come to bear.
People dwell in lonely hollows
Upon forgotten hills,
Unaware of One to love them
The Shepherd of the hills.
Unheard, His words "I'll come to you"
Unaware, His divine joy,
Flooding darkness with His light
Jesus evermore.

*"The LORD is my shepherd;
I shall not want."*

Psalms 23:1

Let Me Glory
in Each Day

On a glorious day that God has made
His loving kindness I let fade,
My thoughts on things I did not need
From His Holy Word I did not feed.
A day I closed in weariness
Aware of joyful moments missed,
Distraught thoughts not overcome
Good deeds lost I could have done.
I am thankful God has let me see
My thoughts were focused back on me,
To crowd my service to His need
To still the voice I need to heed.
Let me not selfishly again
Forget this earth and all therein,
Are made by His love for happy living
Redeemed by pain and all forgiving
Let me glory in each day
Rejoice with eyes upon God's way.

*"This is the day which the LORD hath made;
we will rejoice and be glad in it."*

Psalm 118:24

Psalm 32

Blessed is he whose transgression
is forgiven,
whose sin is covered.
Blessed is the man unto whom
the LORD imputeth not iniquity,
and in whose spirit there is no guile.
When I kept silence,
my bones waxed old through my roaring
all the day long.
For day and night thy hand was
heavy upon me:
my moisture is turned into the
drought of summer.
I acknowledged my sin unto thee,
and mine iniquity have I not hid.
I said, I will confess my transgressions
unto the LORD;
and thou forgavest the iniquity of my sin.
For this shall every one that is godly pray
unto thee in a time when thou
mayest be found:
surely in the floods of great waters they
shall not come nigh unto him.
Thou art my hiding place;
thou shalt preserve me from trouble;

thou shalt compass me
about with songs of deliverance.
I will instruct thee
and teach thee in the way which
thou shalt go:
I will guide thee with mine eye.
Be ye not as the horse,
or as the mule, which have no
understanding:
whose mouth must be held in with
bit and bridle,
lest they come near unto thee.
Many sorrows shall be to the wicked:
but he that trusteth in the LORD,
mercy shalt compass him about.
Be glad in the LORD,
and rejoice, ye righteous:
and shout for joy,
all ye that are upright in heart.

Why Stand Alone

Alone and in confusion
We need God's guiding hand,
To lead us through the many things
We do not understand.
And though we may not see the way
God is answering our prayers,
We cannot doubt His presence
And the fact He really cares.
Prayer is a lifetime process
Step-by-step each hour, each day,
And involves the kind of faith
That trusts completely in God's way.
Though His answers may be different
His time not what we'd choose,
His patient love and wisdom
True assurance we'll not lose.
God's love will last forever
When all else is gone,
Place your faith in His good grace
And you will never stand alone.

*"Jesus saith unto him, Thomas, because thou
hast seen me, thou hast believed: blessed are
they that have not seen, and yet have believed."*

John 20:29

By the Way of the Cross

Jesus walked by the way of the Cross
And made a place for all to go,
To unload the heavy burden of sin
And to find the love we need so.
A place to know there is One to care
Who sees, Who hears, Who knows,
Great with mercy and kindness
A place where His love ever flows.
He bids a welcome to His sacred place
To all who have no place to grow,
Come taste the love of Our Father
You will rejoice it is Christ
that you know.
From the Cross He paved a pathway
That leads to our Father above,
So that where Christ is, we also will be
Forever in eternal love.

"Who hath ears to hear, let him hear."

Matthew 13:9

Reaching Hands

The hands that calm the waters
Beneath a ship on stormy sea,
The hands that sealed the lion's mouth
So Daniel could go free.
The hands that healed the leprosy
Caused blinded eyes to see,
The hands that touched the crippled
As He walked in Galilee,
The hands that bear the nail scars
And that bled unceasingly,
The hands that called forth Lazarus
Bade to all, "Come follow Me,"
Are the hands stretched forth today
Reaching out to you and me!

*" . . . I am the resurrection, and the life:
he that believeth in me, though he were dead,
yet shall he live: And whosoever liveth
and believeth in me shall never die.
Believest thou this?"*

John 11: 25–26

Psalm 113

Praise ye the LORD. Praise, O ye servants
of the LORD, praise the name
of the LORD.
Blessed be the name of the LORD from
this time forth and for evermore.
From the rising of the sun unto the going
down of the same the LORD's
name is to be praised.
The LORD is high above all nations,
and his glory above the heavens.
Who is like unto the LORD our God,
who dwelleth on high,
Who humbleth himself to behold the
things that are in heaven, and in the earth!
He raiseth up the poor out of the dust,
and lifteth the needy out of the dunghill;
That he may set him with princes,
even with the princes of his people.
He maketh the barren woman
to keep house,
and to be a joyful mother of children.
Praise ye the LORD.

God Is My Refuge

God is my refuge
In the midst of life's storms,
God is my fortress, a rose
In bloom o'er the thorns.
His love rests inside me
He safeguards my trust,
My walk with Him daily
I find is a must.
Forever He's near me
A presence felt dear,
He lightens my heartaches
He cushions all fear.
My soul waits in silence
For God's hand to guide me,
My heart feels His quietness
Whatever betides me.
Forever He hears me
Above roarings of man,
Forever He strengthens
Whatever His plan.
Whenever I falter
He alone understands,
He holds all my hope safely
In the palm of His hand.

*"Come unto me, all ye that labour
and are heavy laden, and I will give you rest."*

Matthew 11:28

Simply With Jesus

Lead me to the simple life
To do lovely simple things,
Let me own a simple heart
That loving simply brings.
Treasure deep a simple smile
A simple caring deed,
Know the joy of simply giving
To keep me from a heart of greed.
Embrace a morning sunrise
In simple quiet solitude,
Let me dine upon simplicity
To gain a simple loving attitude.
It begins with loving Jesus
See Him in all I say and do,
Let love bring to me a simple life
A grand MAJESTIC VIEW.

"The law of the LORD is perfect,
converting the soul:
the testimony of the LORD
is sure, making wise the simple."

Psalm 19:7

An Eternal Arm

The pain of human suffering
Continues on and on,
Even when the reasons
Are still to us unknown.
God asks us not to lean upon
The way we understand,
Through prayer allow His will be done
And to hold on to His hand.
For He will guide us through
All in life that comes our way,
Till that bright and glorious time
When we will understand TODAY.
So, when you do not understand
Lean upon His eternal Arm,
God's Word can calm a raging sea
And still a mighty storm.

"They that sow in tears shall reap in joy."

Psalm 126:5

I Cry Out, Lord, To Thee

Grant to me Your wisdom
For my troubled heart to see,
A full measure of Your wealth unfold
When I cry out, Lord, to Thee.
I want to be a caring child
Each day to, "Be ye kind,"
To come to know Your change in me
In my heart and in my mind.
Let me lose my selfish ways
To gain more and more of You,
Pray You open wide the windows
With rich blessings flowing through.
For all the wealth on earth below
Does naught to set me free,
Pour out today upon my heart
Wealth that comes from only Thee.

*"The LORD knoweth the
days of the upright:
and their inheritance shall be for ever."*

Psalm 37:18

One Little Candle

One little candle
Will give a light to see,
Shine forth into the darkness
To glow for you and me.
From one little candle
God can magnify the glow,
To lighten other places
As His Son we come to know.
When the storms and ill winds come
A lashing wind can blow,
Through it all our light will shine
And will forever flow.
With our light held high and bright
To all the world we'll show,
It is the mighty power of prayer
That fuels the candle's glow.

*"Unto the upright there ariseth light in the
darkness: he is gracious,
and full of compassion, and righteous."*

Psalm 112:4

Sow Your Light Upon My Pathway

Make Your Spirit strong within me
Lord, hold tightly to my hand,
Let me know the path I take
Guides me forth by Your command.
Sow Your light upon my pathway
Clear the way You have for me,
Hear my prayer, O Lord, this day
Let my soul rest quiet with Thee.
You're my hope, my peace, my joy,
and my life
Your glory shines before me,
Your way endures forever
And it's forever I'll need Thee.
Let me feel Your breath upon me
As you teach me what to say,
It is then I'll know my footsteps
Leads me to Your perfect way.

*"And he said, My presence shall go with thee,
and I will give thee rest."*

Exodus 33:14

I See the Mountain Tops

I am standing on a mountain
I see afar another
Down below and in between
Is a valley I must cover.
I struggled up this mountain
At times I had to rest,
I walked with strength and courage
For my God I did my best.
I will go down this mountain
With an easy stride
I will struggle through the valley
I will reach the other side.
I will climb another mountain
I will reach another peak
For it is God's love and guidance
That leads to Him, the One I seek.

*"For the LORD shall be thy confidence,
and shall keep thy foot from being taken."*

Proverbs 3:26

God Has a Pathway

A new life begins a pathway
God hopes for us to trod,
Each day a blessed event
When our path is led by God.
Our Creator has a purpose
For every grain of sand,
For every ray of light that shines
So bright upon this land.
For every golden leaf that falls
And every ocean wave,
The whistle of the wind we hear
A purpose our God gave.
Every gentle blade of grass
The blended colors of the sea,
Not a single cloud up in the sky
God did not mean to be.
For every tree so high that stands
A fragrant breath of a rose,
For every drop of rain that falls
Its purpose our God knows.
Each step we take upon His path
And when our path will end,
Is our great Creator's plan
It all begins and ends with Him.

"He giveth snow like wool:
he scattereth the hoarfrost like ashes.
He casteth forth his ice like morsels:
who can stand before his cold?
He sendeth out his word,
and melteth them:
he causeth his wind to blow,
and the waters flow.

Psalm 147:16–18

Fresh Raindrops

Let our hearts sing with gladness
For we work not in vain,
When we are led by the Spirit
So much He'll attain.
For there are roses and daffodils
And buttercups, small
Plants to be watered
Trees to grow tall.
There are streams to flourish
When fresh raindrops fall
Overflowing the rivers
A soul's wake-up call.
Deserts to conquer
Mountains to scale,
In the way of the Spirit
There is naught to fail.
Sing songs in the pastures
Laugh from the hills,
There is joy in fresh raindrops
Rejoice in the good of God's will.

"I have not spoken in secret,
in a dark place of the earth:
I said not unto the seed of Jacob,
Seek ye me in vain:

I the LORD speak righteousness,
I declare things that are right."

Isaiah 45:19

God Makes a Difference

Lord, I want to make a difference
To a hurting friend,
I want to find a way to say
The pain will surely end.
Broken hearts are mended
Hope will spring anew,
All because there's One to care
Your love is tried and true.
Sad spirits can be brightened
With smile to light a face,
When one learns to recognize
And know Your loving grace.
Like many of Your children
I know what You can do,
I want to touch a hurting friend
For I was hurting, too.

"These things I have spoken unto you,
that in me ye might have peace.
In the world ye shall have tribulation:
but be of good cheer;
I have overcome the world."

John 16—33

God is on Our Side

(Our Nation's Heritage Shall Be Forever)

II Chronicles 16:9
"For the eyes of the LORD run to and fro
throughout the whole earth,
to shew himself strong in the behalf
of them whose
heart is perfect toward him.
Herein thou hast done foolishly:
therefore from henceforth thou
shalt have wars."

II Chronicles 7:14
"If my people, which are called by my name,
shall humble themselves,
and pray,
and seek my face,
and turn from their wicked ways;
then will I hear from heaven,
and will forgive their sin,
and will heal their land."

II Chronicles 14:11

" . . . LORD, it is nothing with thee to help,
whether with many,
or with them that have no power:
help us, O LORD our God;
for we rest on thee,
and in thy name we go against this multitude.
O LORD, thou art our God;
let not man prevail against thee."

Psalm 127:1

" EXCEPT the LORD build the house,
they labour in vain that build it:
except the LORD keep the city,
the watchman waketh but in vain."

A Prayer for You

"And this I pray,
that your love may abound yet more
and more in knowledge and in all judgment;
That ye may approve things that are excellent;
that ye may be sincere and without
offence till the day of Christ;
Being filled with the fruits of righteousness,
which are by Jesus Christ,
unto the glory and praise of God."

Philippians 1:9–11

"Call unto me, and I will answer thee,
and shew thee great and mighty things,
which thou knowest not."

Jeremiah 33:3

Epilogue

In Memory Of
(A wonderful brother)
James "Mal" Malcolm Faircloth
July 2, 1938–September 7, 2005

"Sorrow is better than laughter:
for by the sadness of the countenance the
heart is made better."

Ecclesiastes 7:3

An Awareness of Sorrow

Waves of sorrow flowing free
Rushing through our soul,
We turn our thoughts upon the One
Whose hand is in control.
Through tearful eyes that cannot see
We feel God's presence near,
As earnestly we seek Him
And His promises so dear.
We know He will touch the sadness
His awareness made anew,
As we seek His strength and courage
Our hearts He will renew.
His love is like a miracle
A light when life is dark,
In remembrance, we will trust Him
As He grants to all a better heart.

"Thank you, Mal, for leaving
behind a most beautiful gift from
God to each of us,
a better heart."

About the Author

Sherry Faircloth Skinner was born in Asheville, North Carolina, and moved to Jacksonville, Florida, at an early age, where she now resides with her husband, Marvin. They have been blessed with two sons and three grandchildren. Her greatest enjoyments are her time with her grandchildren, reading her Bible, needlepoint, and the beautiful beaches of Florida. Sherry's personal ministry is sharing her work as Christ leads.

Contact author Sherry Faircloth Skinner
or order more copies of this book at

TATE PUBLISHING, LLC

127 East Trade Center Terrace
Mustang, Oklahoma 73064

(888) 361 - 9473

Tate Publishing, LLC

www.tatepublishing.com